LOOK AND SEE ³

ACTIVITY BOOK

NATIONAL GEOGRAPHIC
LEARNING

Australia • Brazil • Mexico • Singapore • United Kingdom • United States

BACK TO SCHOOL

1 **TR: 0.1** Listen and match. Then say.

1 2 3 4

MONDAY	TUESDAY	WEDNESDAY	THURSDAY
1	2	3	4

FRIDAY	SATURDAY	SUNDAY
5	6	7

STRUCTURE: *What day is it today? It's Monday.*

IN CLASS

1 TR: 1.1 Listen. Circle ✔ or ✗.

1 (✔) ✗

2 ✔ ✗

3 ✔ ✗

4 ✔ ✗

5 ✔ ✗

6 ✔ ✗

7 ✔ ✗

2 Point and say.

NEW WORDS: *count to ten, draw a picture, make a craft, play a game, read a book, sing a song, write letters*

1 TR: **1.2** Listen and match. Then point and say.

1 2 3 4 5 6 7

1 TR: 1.3 Find and say. Then listen and sing.

2 Write ✔ or ✗.

VALUE **WORK HARD AT SCHOOL.**

1 ☐

2 ☐

3 ☐

1 TR: 1.4 Listen and trace. Say.

1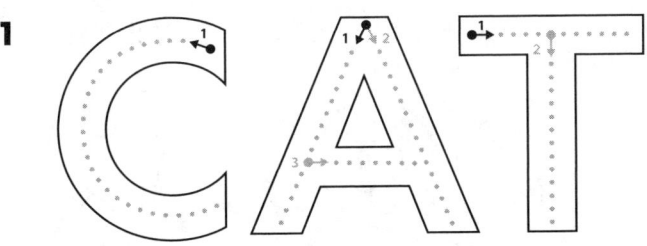

CAT

2

RAT

2 Trace.

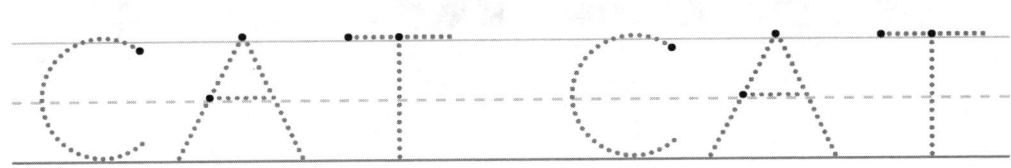

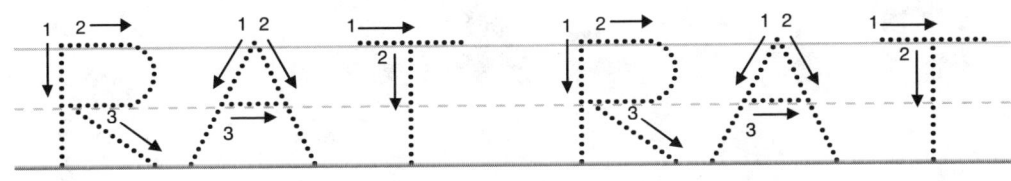

1 Match. Color and say.

$9 + 1 = 10$

$3 + 1 = 4$

$5 + 1 = 6$

VIDEO: SC: 2 *(optional)* **Content Words:** *add, cupcake, more*

STRUCTURE: *Is he/she a doctor? Yes, he/she is./No, he/she isn't.*

1 TR: 3.3 Listen and color.

2 Write ✔ or ✘.

 VALUE   BE POLITE.

1

2

3

2 Trace.

1

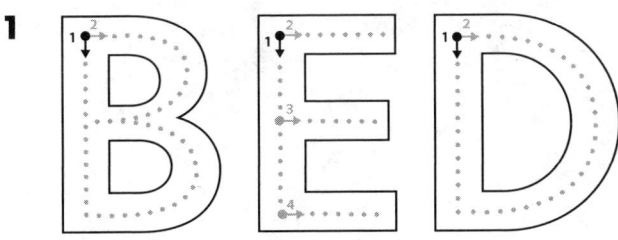

BED

2

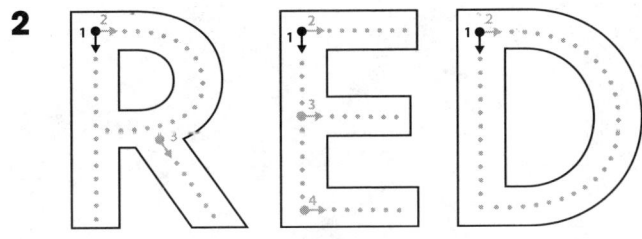

RED

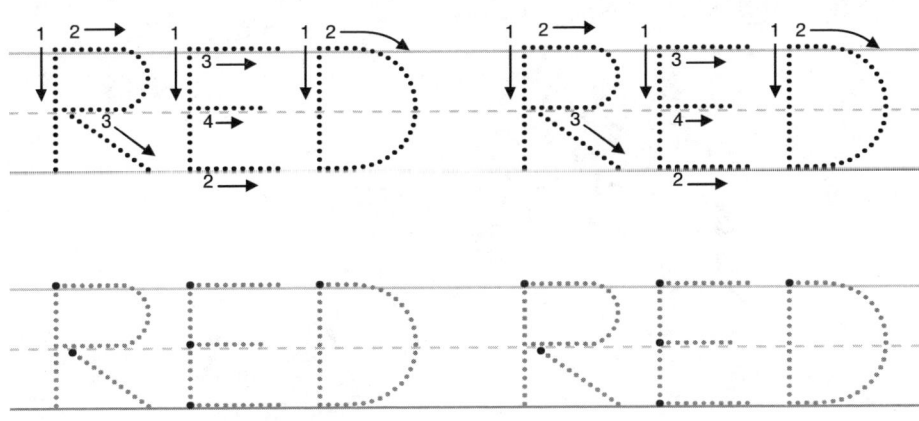

1 TR: 3.5 Listen and point. Then say.

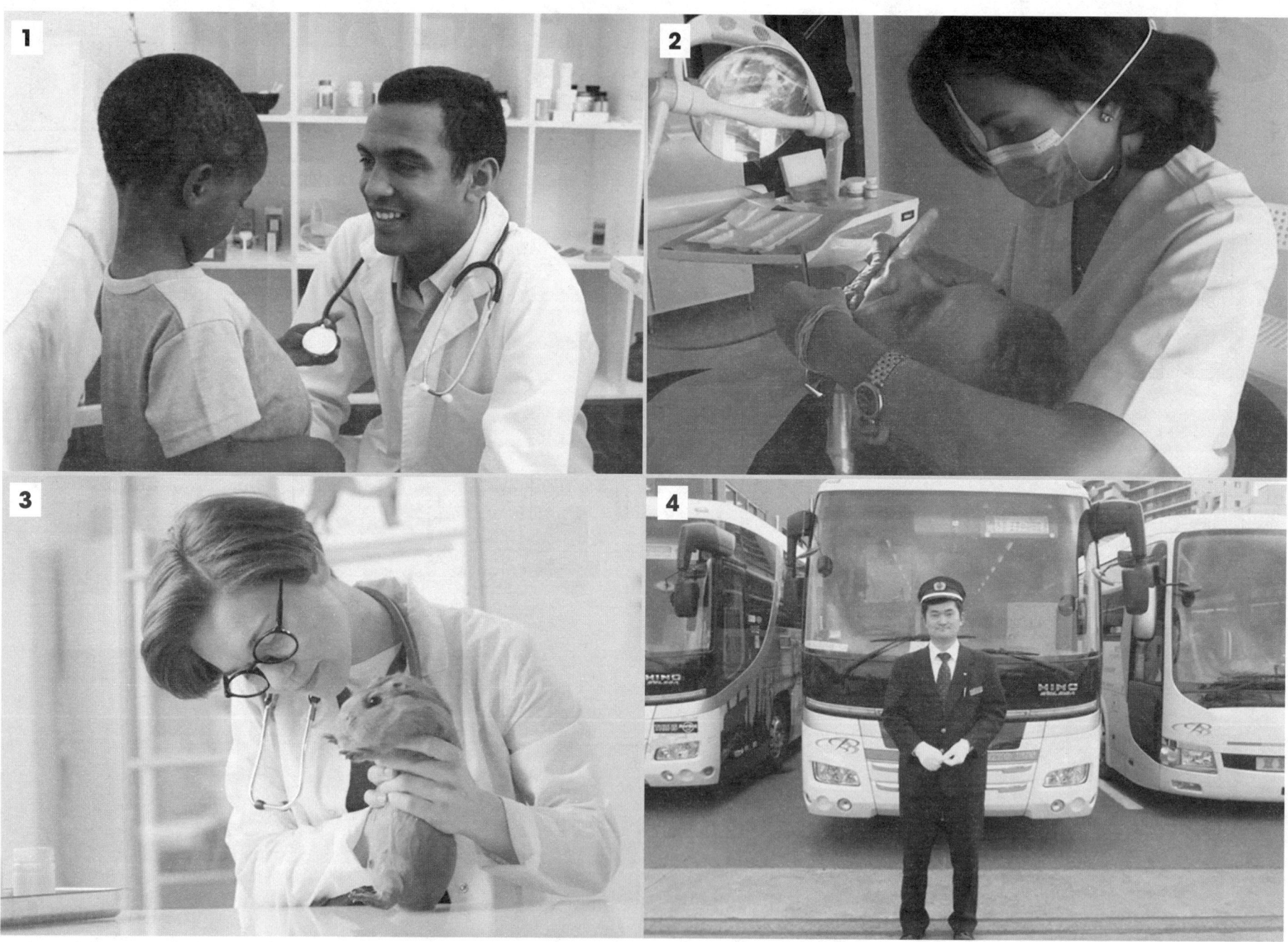

1

2

3

4

VIDEO: SC: 6 *(optional)* **Content Words:** *help, people*

REVIEW: NEW WORDS: *bus driver, dentist, doctor, firefighter, librarian, mail carrier, police officer, vet*
STRUCTURE: *Is he/she a doctor? Yes, he/she is./No, he/she isn't.*

21

UNIT 4 MAKE SOME NOISE!

1 TR: 4.1 Listen. Write ✔ or ✗.

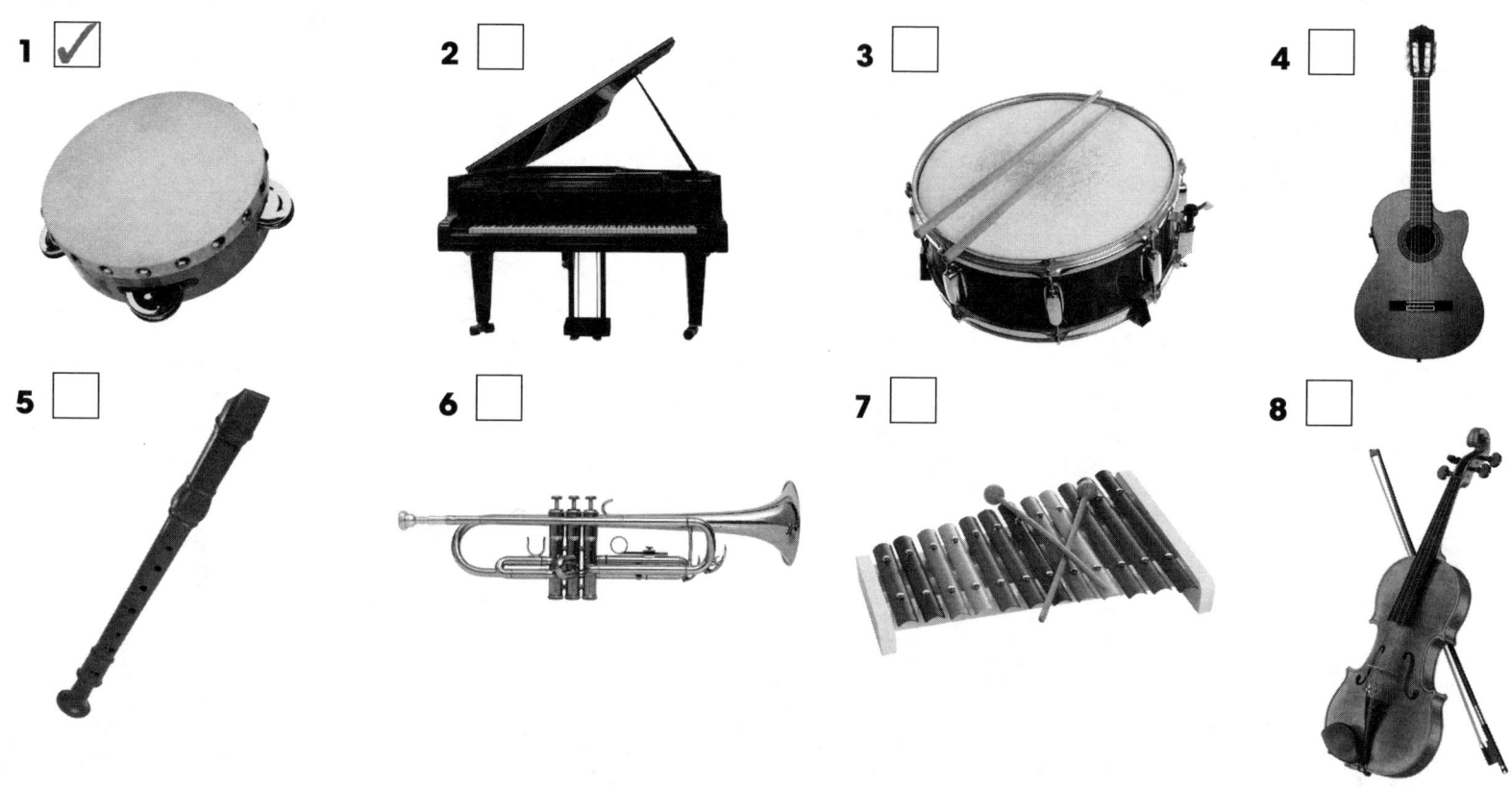

1 ✔
2 ☐
3 ☐
4 ☐
5 ☐
6 ☐
7 ☐
8 ☐

2 Point and say.

NEW WORDS: *drums, guitar, piano, recorder, tambourine, trumpet, violin, xylophone*

STRUCTURE: *He can play the piano. She can play the guitar.*

23

1 TR: 4.3 Listen and circle. Then sing and point.

2 Write ✔ or ✗.

VALUE   **WORK TOGETHER.**

1 ☐

2 ☐

3 ☐

STRUCTURE: *Is he/she a doctor? Yes, he/she is./No, he/she isn't.*

17

1 TR: 3.3 Listen and color.

2 Write ✔ or ✘.

1

2

3

1 Listen and trace. Say.

1

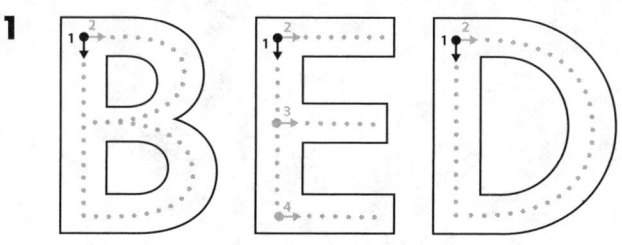

BED

2

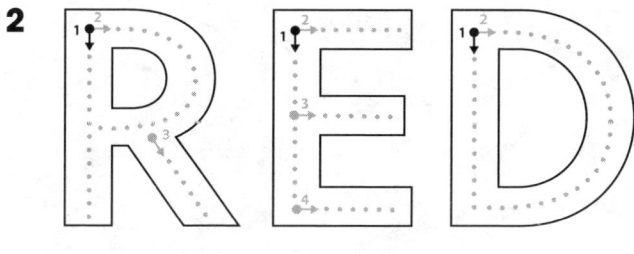

RED

2 Trace.

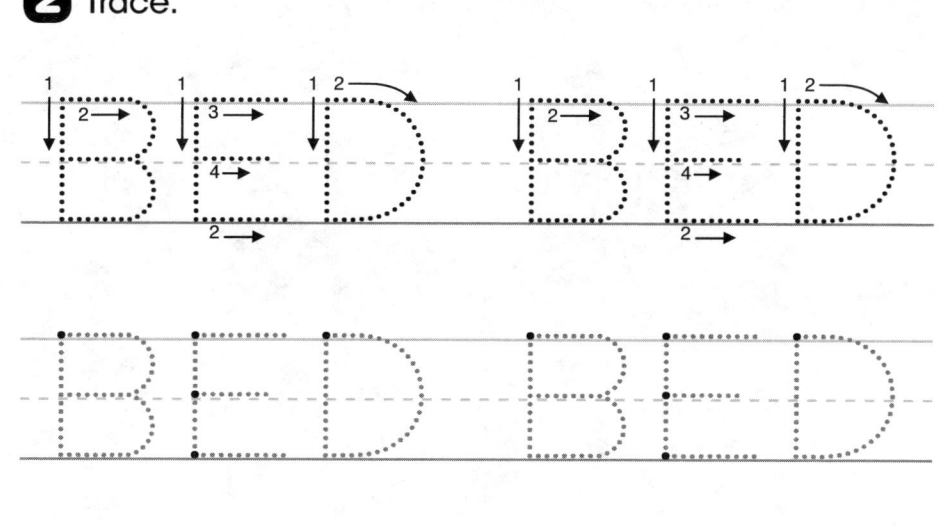

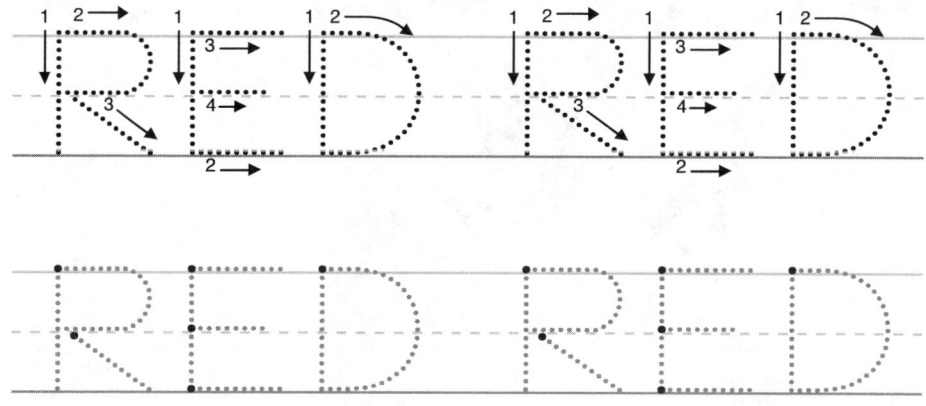

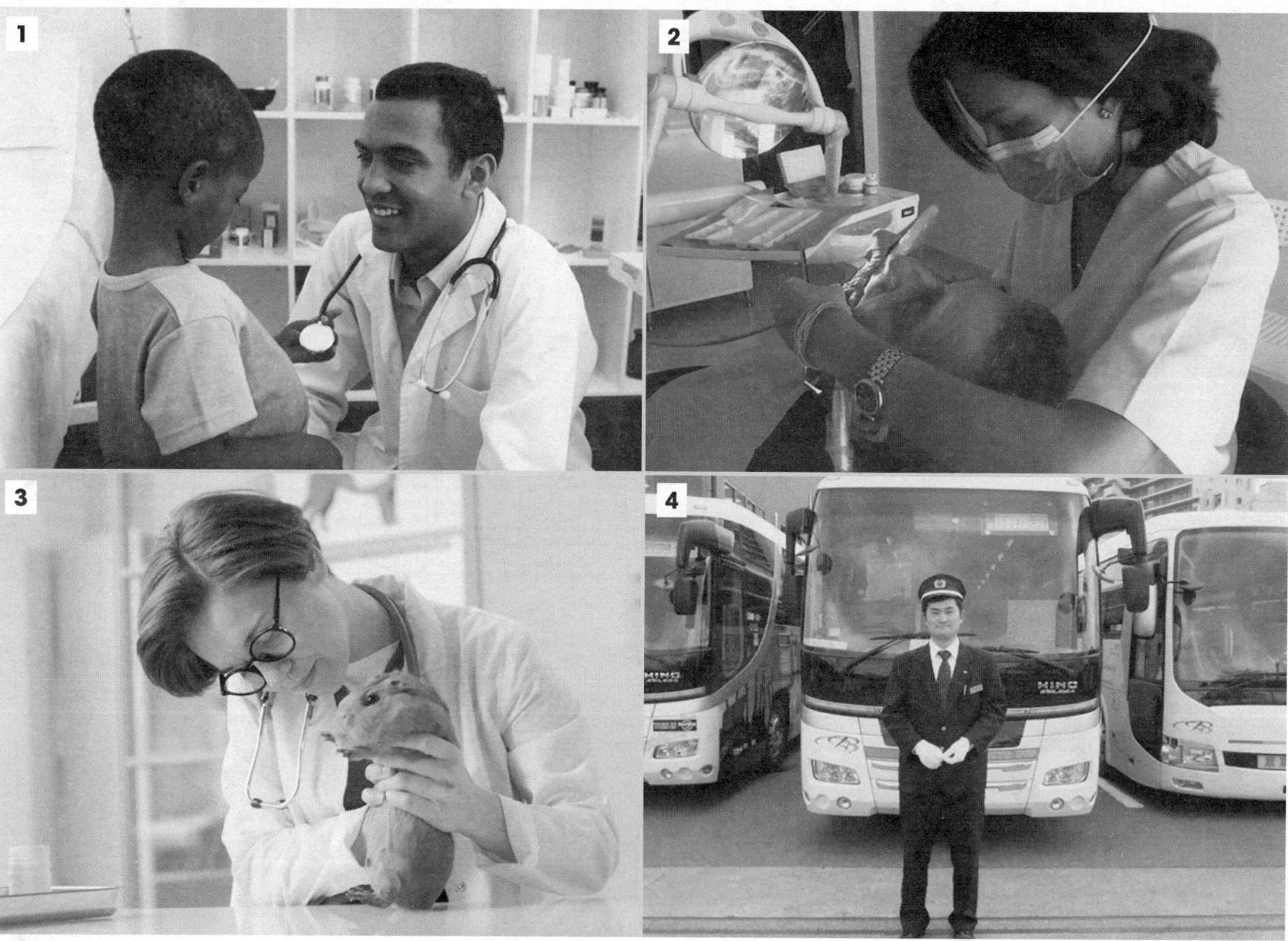

VIDEO: SC: 6 (optional)   **Content Words:** *help, people*

1 TR: 3.6 Listen and match. Then say.

1 2 3 4 5 6 7 8

REVIEW: NEW WORDS: *bus driver, dentist, doctor, firefighter, librarian, mail carrier, police officer, vet*
STRUCTURE: *Is he/she a doctor? Yes, he/she is./No, he/she isn't.*

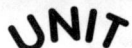

UNIT 4

MAKE SOME NOISE!

1 TR: 4.1 Listen. Write ✔ or ✘.

1 ✔

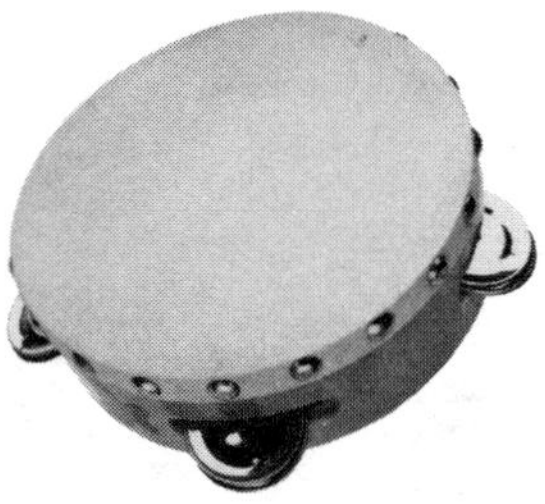

2 ☐

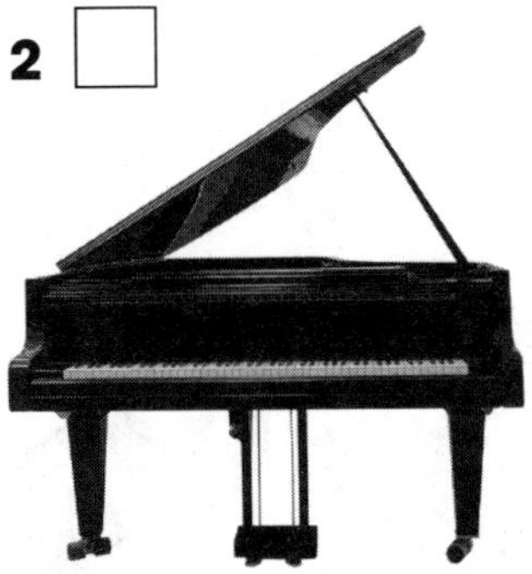

3 ☐

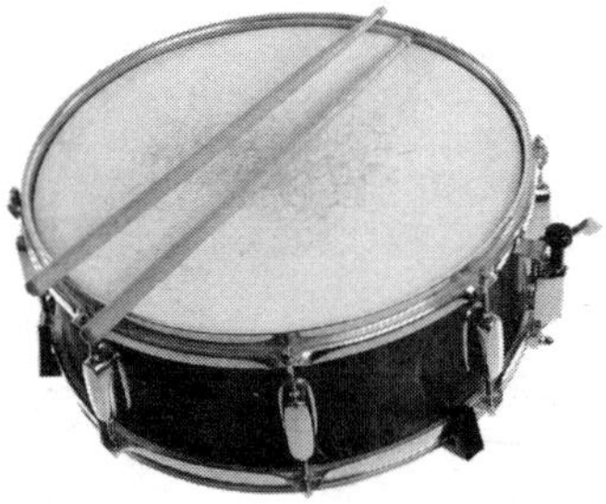

4 ☐

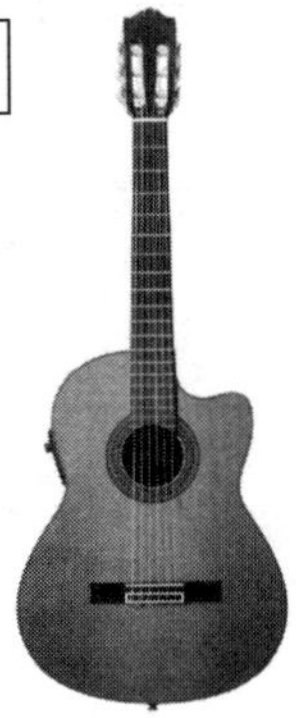

5 ☐

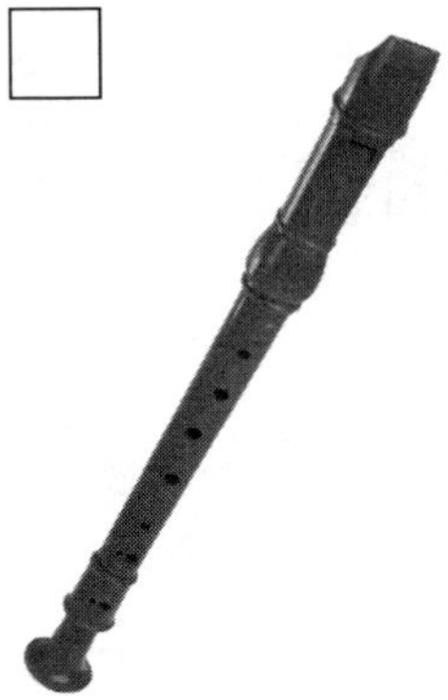

6 ☐

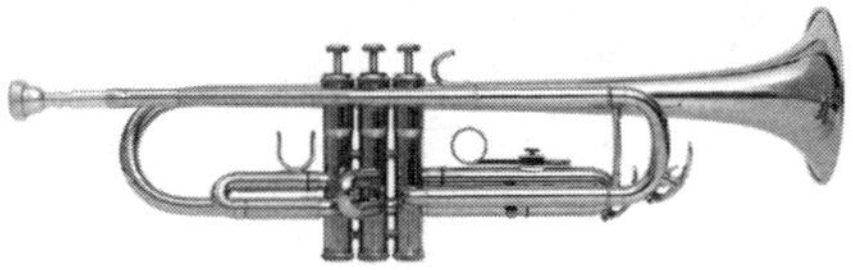

7 ☐

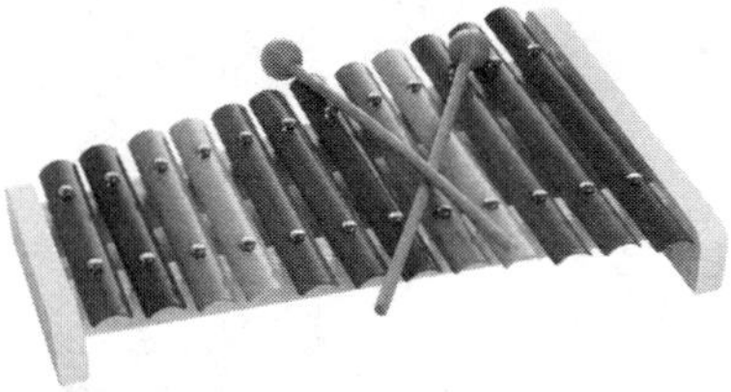

8 ☐

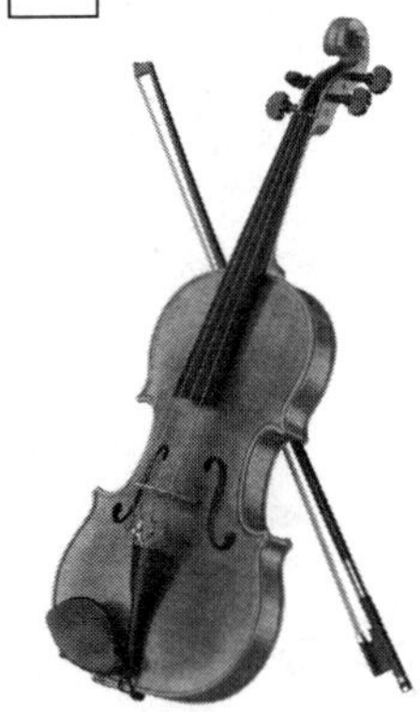

2 Point and say.

NEW WORDS: *drums, guitar, piano, recorder, tambourine, trumpet, violin, xylophone*

STRUCTURE: *He can play the piano. She can play the guitar.*

1 TR: 4.3 Listen and circle. Then sing and point.

2 Write ✔ or ✘.

WORK TOGETHER.

1 ☐

2 ☐

3 ☐

1 TR: 4.4 Listen and trace. Say.

1

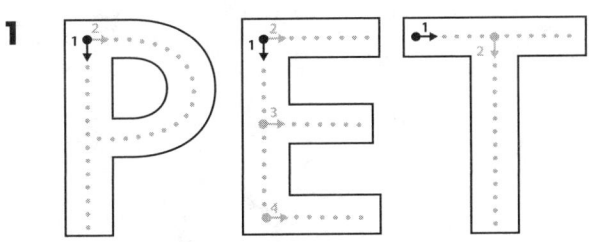

PET

2

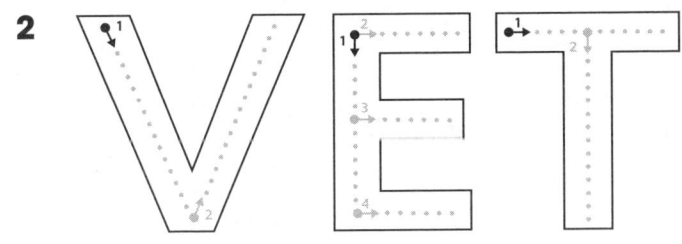

VET

2 Trace.

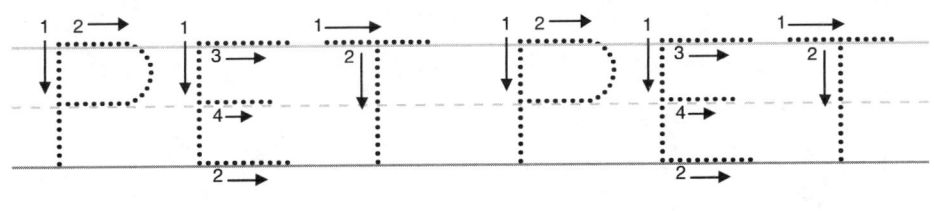

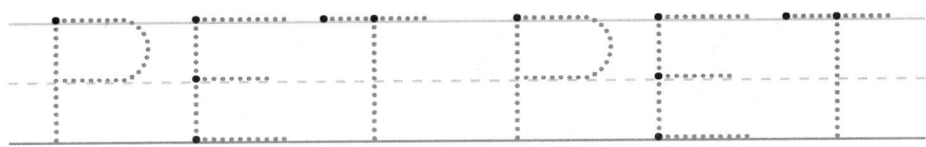

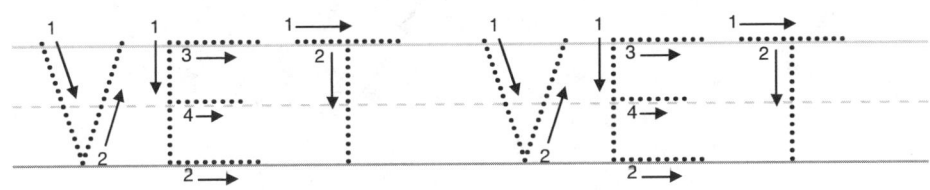

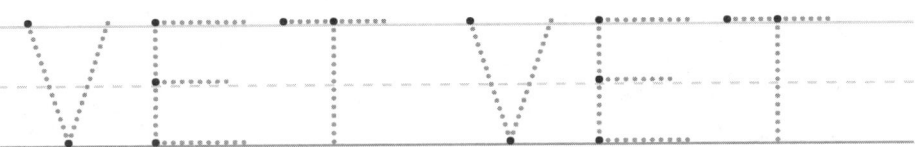

1 Point and say. Then color.

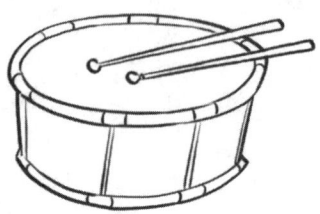

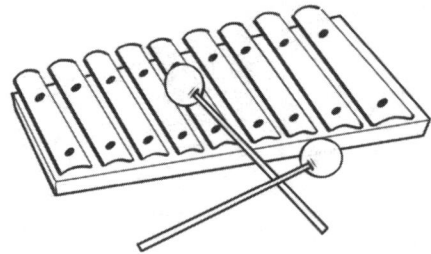

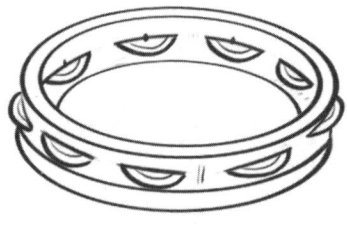

1 Say. Then play and do.

REVIEW: NEW WORDS: *drums, guitar, piano, recorder, tambourine, trumpet, violin, xylophone*
STRUCTURE: *He can play the piano. She can play the guitar.*

27

SHAPES AROUND US

1 TR: 5.1 Listen and match.

1 2 3 4 5 6 7 8

2 Point and say.

NEW WORDS: *circle, diamond, hexagon, oval, rectangle, square, star, triangle*

1 TR: 5.3 Listen and color. Then sing.

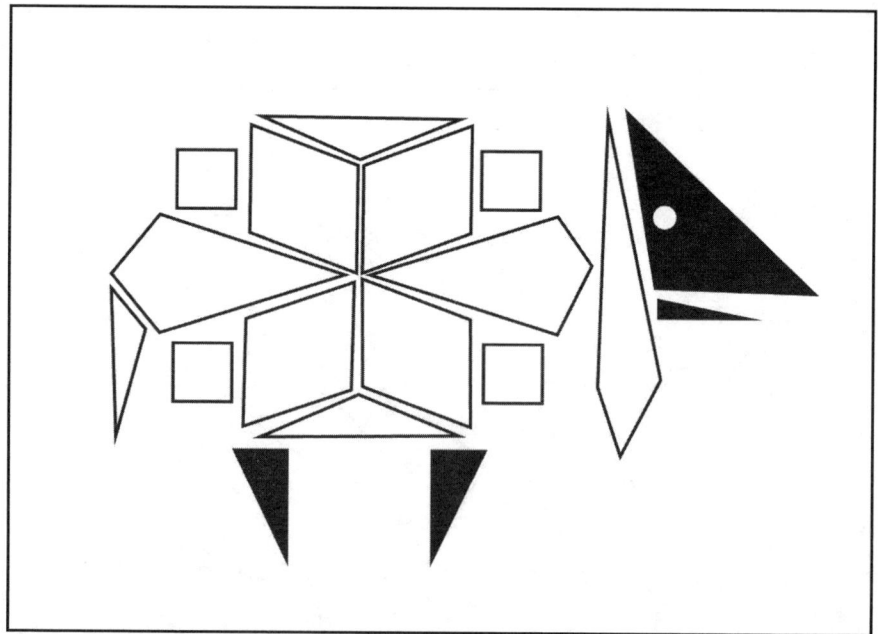

2 Write ✔ or ✘.

USE YOUR IMAGINATION.

1 ☐

2 ☐

3 ☐

1

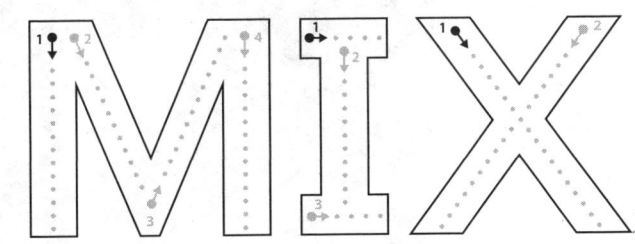

MIX

2

SIX

2 Trace.

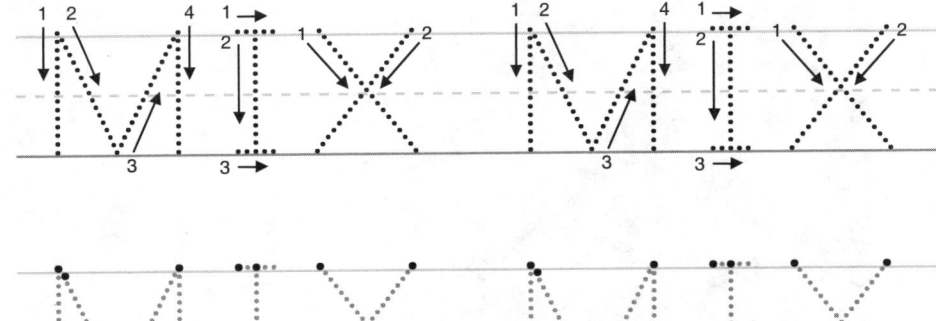

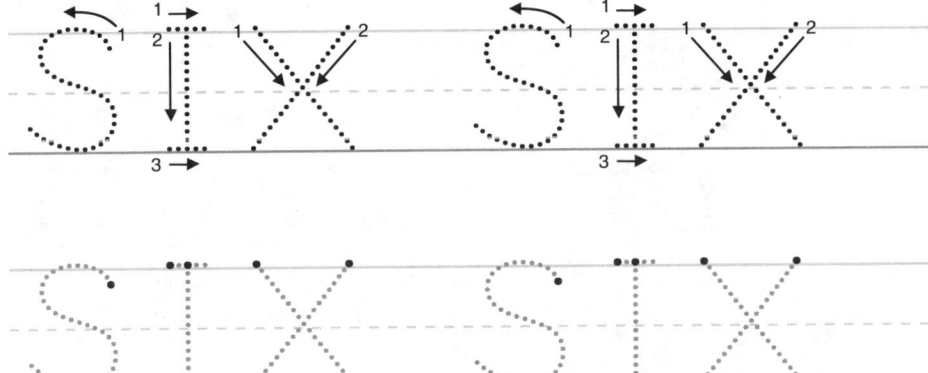

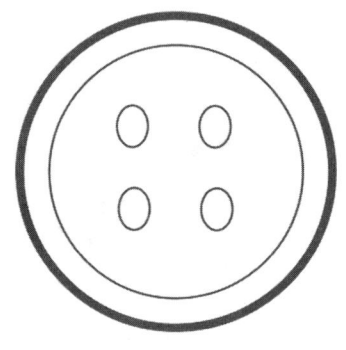

1 Say and color. Then play.

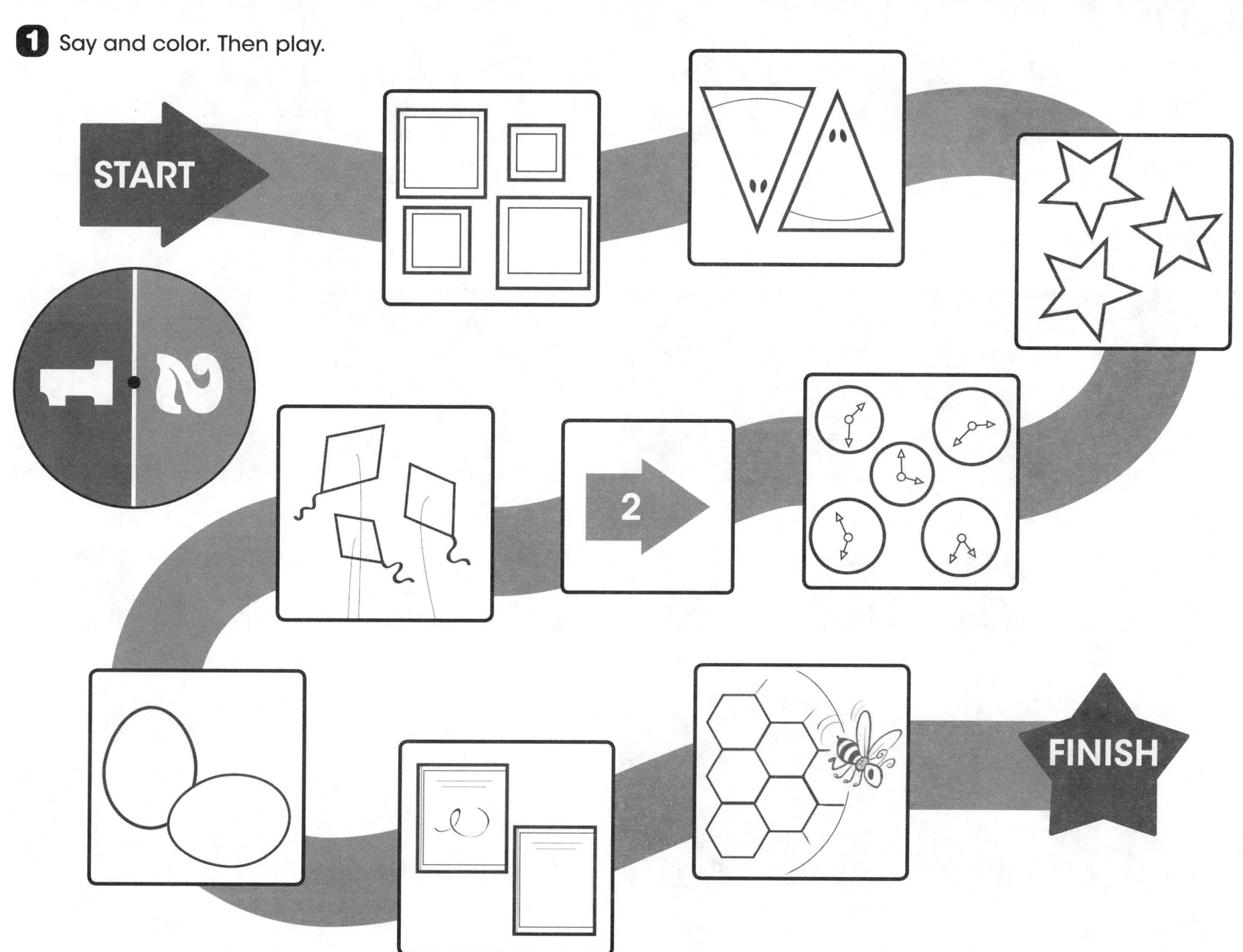

REVIEW: **NEW WORDS:** *circle, diamond, hexagon, oval, rectangle, square, star, triangle*
STRUCTURE: *What are these? They're diamonds.*

33

CAN YOU SWIM?

1 TR: 6.1 Listen and match.

1 2 3 4 5 6 7 8

2 Point and say.

NEW WORDS: *catch, climb, fly, kick, ride, skip, swim, throw*

STRUCTURE: *Can you skip? Yes, I can./No, I can't.*

1 TR: 6.3 Listen and color.

2 Write ✔ or ✗.

1 ☐

2 ☐

3 ☐

1 TR: 6.4 Listen and trace. Say.

1

BIG

2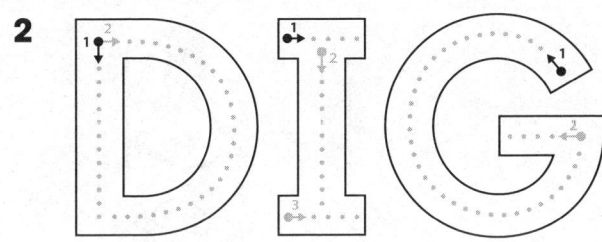

DIG

2 Trace.

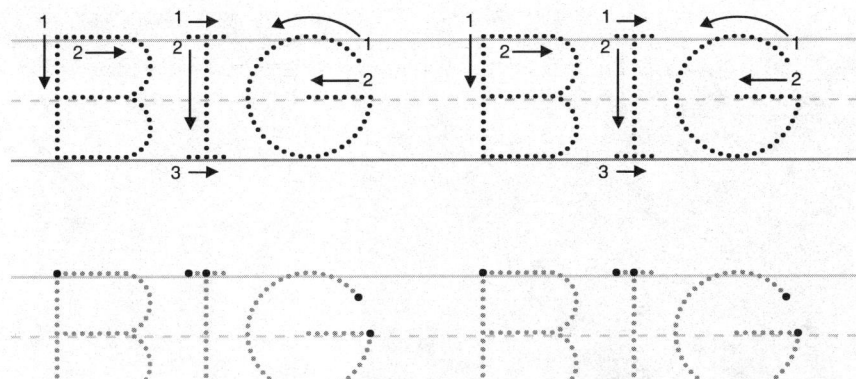

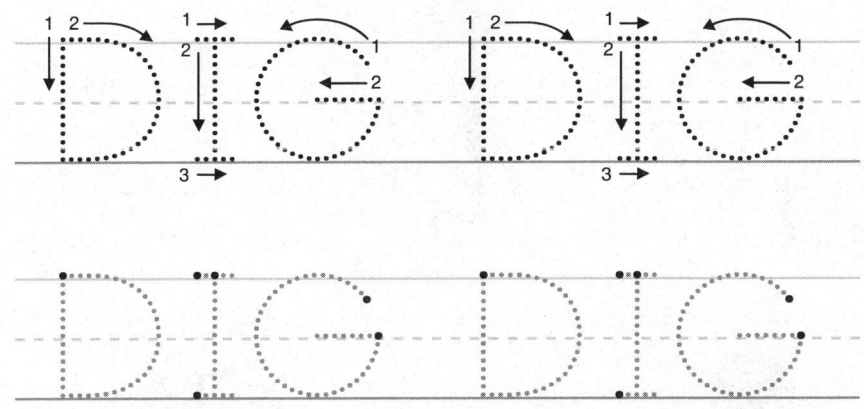

1

2

3

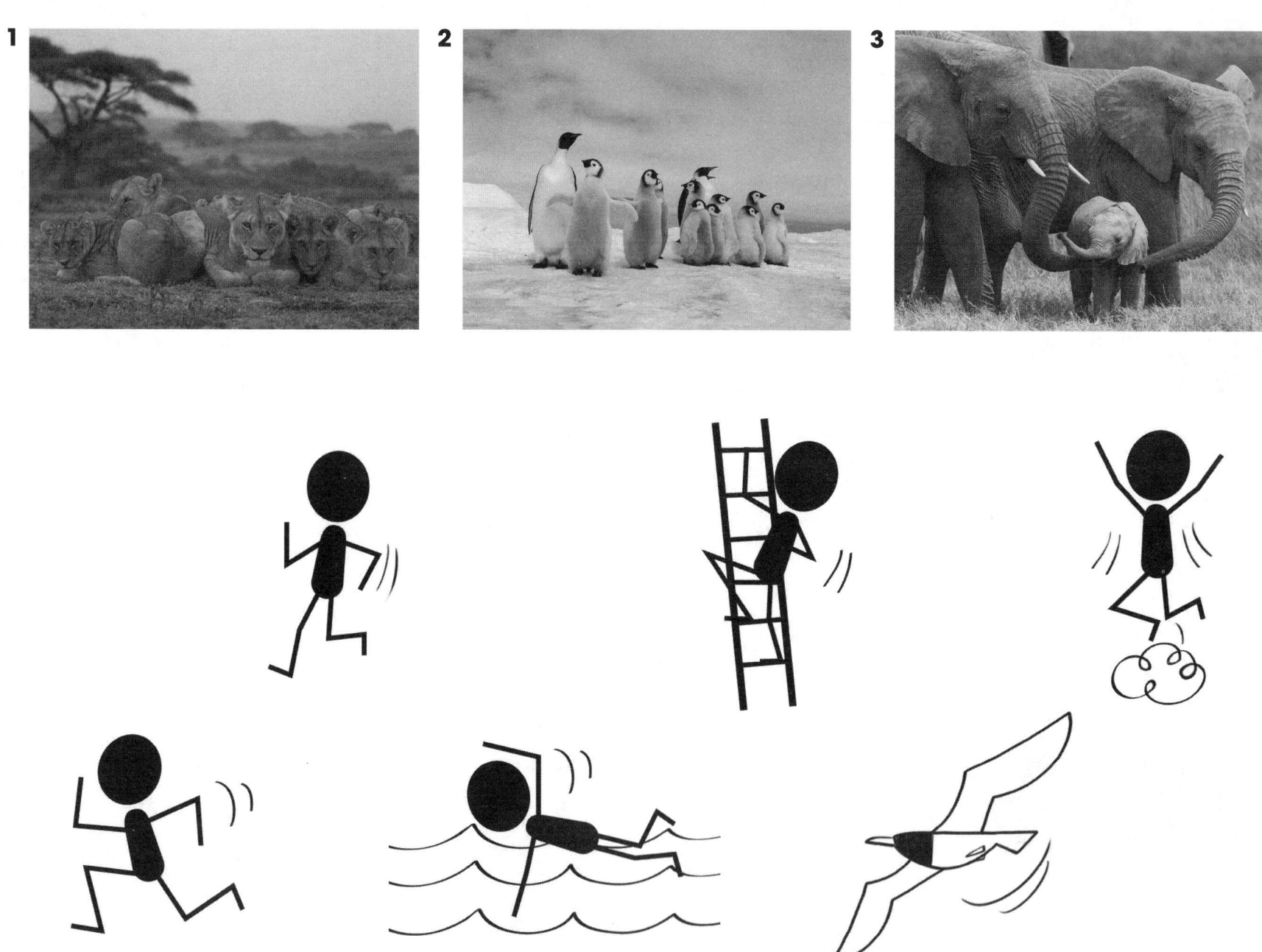

1 Say and color. Then play.

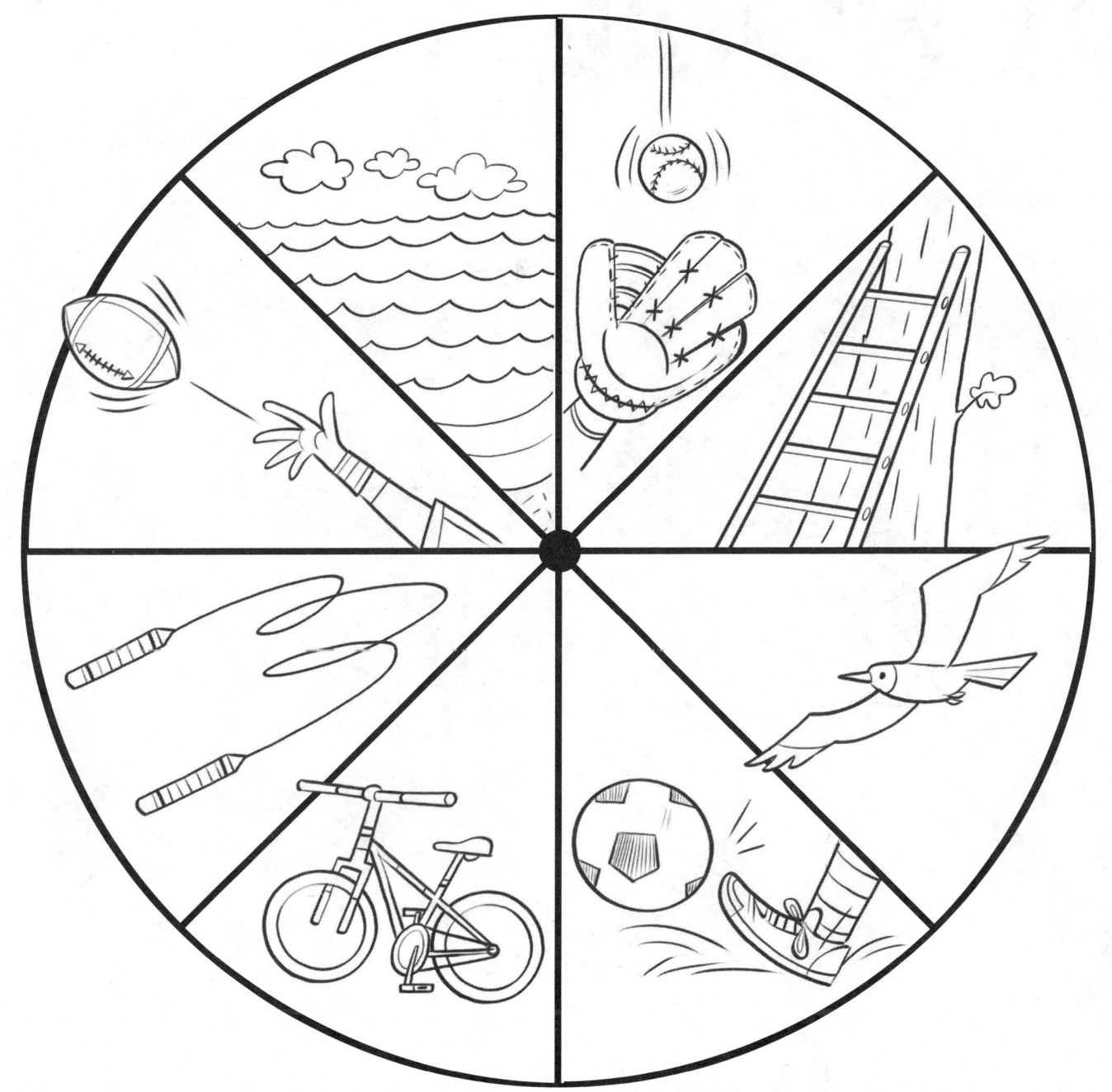

REVIEW: NEW WORDS: *catch, climb, fly, kick, ride, skip, swim, throw*
STRUCTURE: *Can you skip? Yes, I can./No, I can't.*

39

1 TR: 7.1 Listen and circle ✔ or ✘.

1 ✔ ✘

2 ✔ ✘

3 ✔ ✘

4 ✔ ✘

5 ✔ ✘

6 ✔ ✘

7 ✔ ✘

8 ✔ ✘
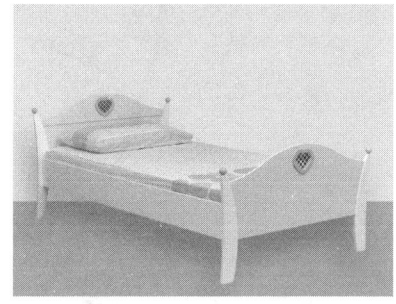

2 Point and say.

NEW WORDS: *bathroom, bedroom, kitchen, living room; bed, shelf, sink, sofa; welcome*

1 TR: 7.2 Listen and match.

1   2   3   4   5   6

STRUCTURE: *The picture is in the bathroom. The cars are under the bed.*

41

1 TR: 7.3 Listen and find. Then sing.

2 Write ✔ or ✘.

VALUE   HELP AT HOME.

1 ☐

2 ☐

3 ☐

1 Listen and trace. Say.

2 Trace.

1

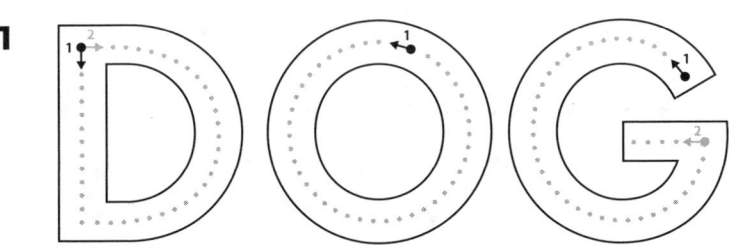

DOG

2

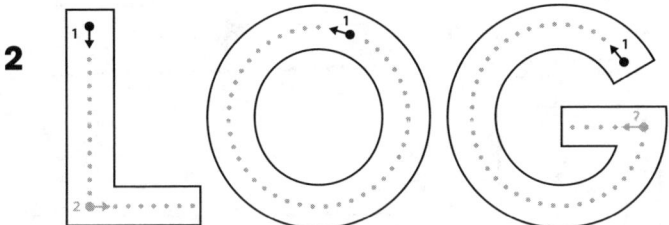

LOG

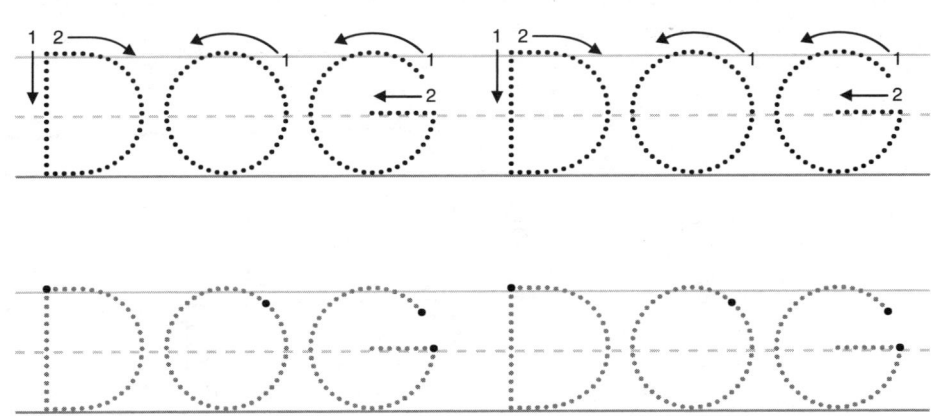

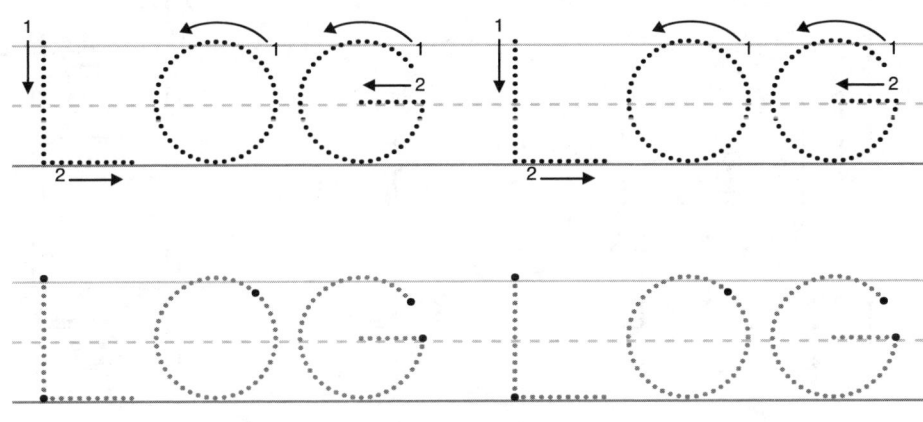

1 Draw and say.

REVIEW: NEW WORDS: *bedroom, bathroom, kitchen, living room; bed, shelf, sink, sofa; welcome*
STRUCTURE: *The picture is in the bathroom. The cars are under the bed.*

45

1 TR: 8.1 Listen. Write ✔ or ✗.

1
2
3
4
5
6
7
8

2 Point and say.

1 What's different? Say.

1

2

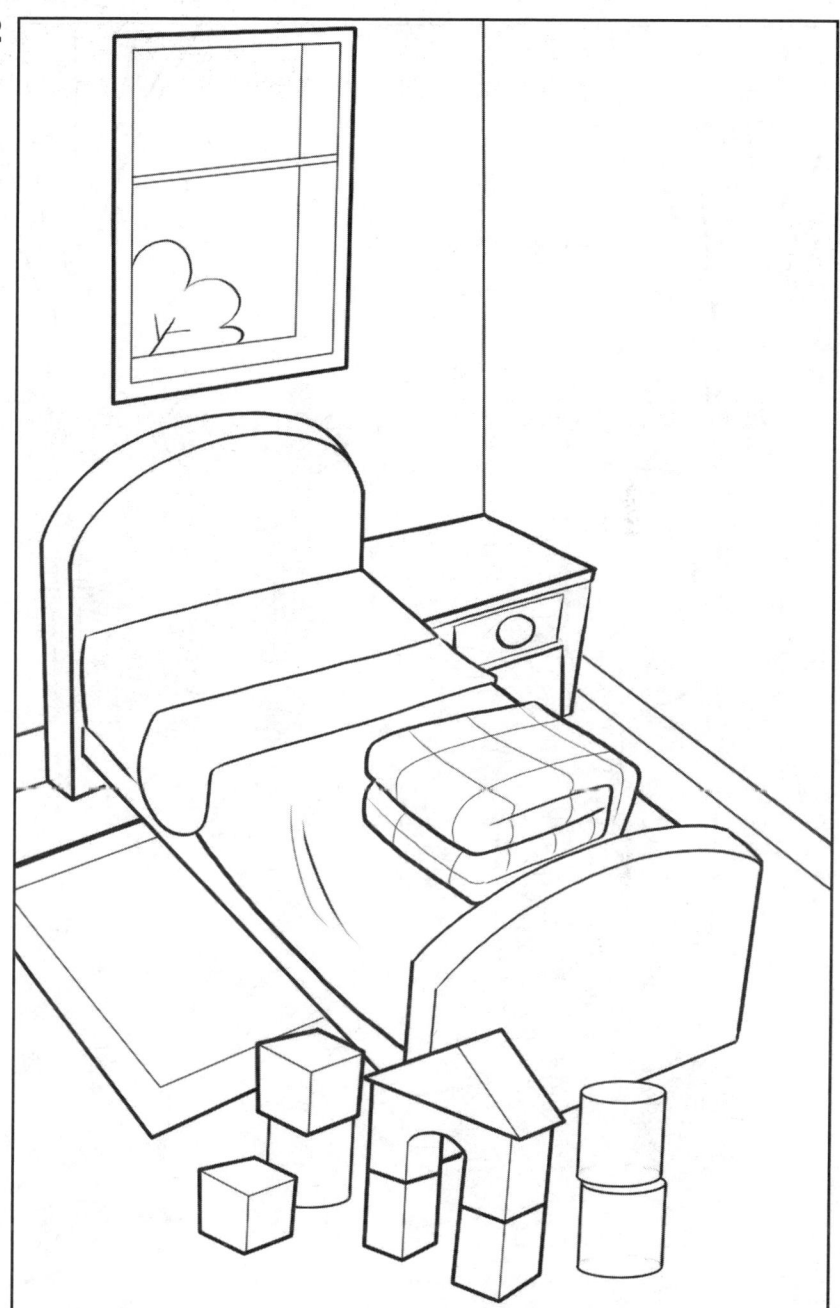

STRUCTURE: *Is there a rug? Yes, there is./No, there isn't.*

1 TR: 8.2 Listen and color.

2 Write ✔ or ✗.

VALUE **BE WELCOMING.**

1

2

3

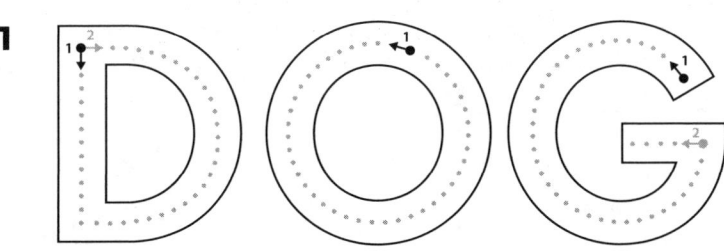

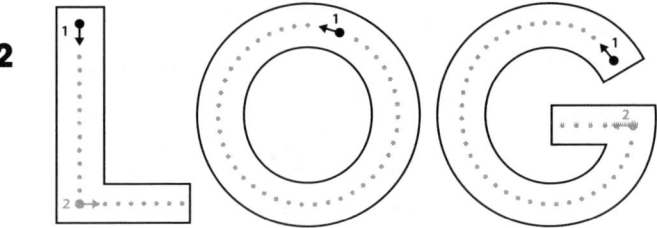

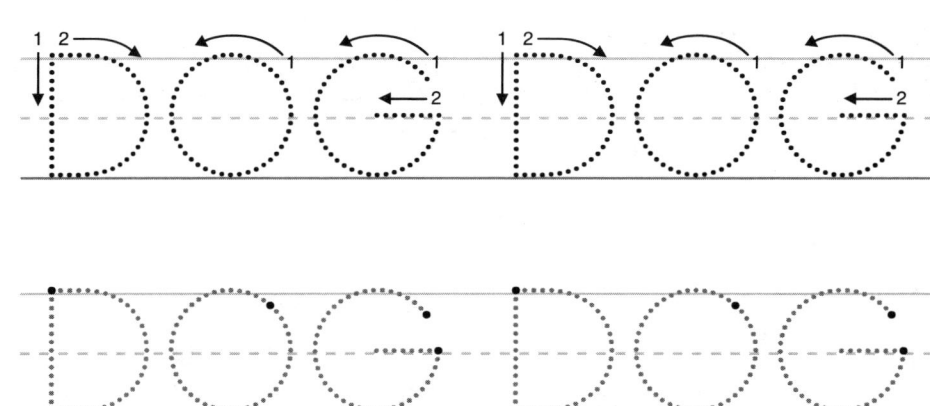

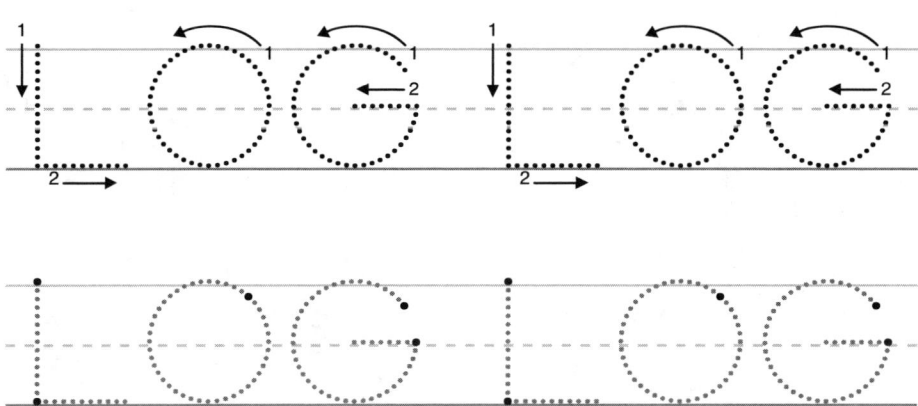

47

1 TR: 8.2 Listen and color.

2 Write ✔ or ✘.

VALUE   BE WELCOMING.

1 ☐

2 ☐

3 ☐

1 Count and say. Then play.

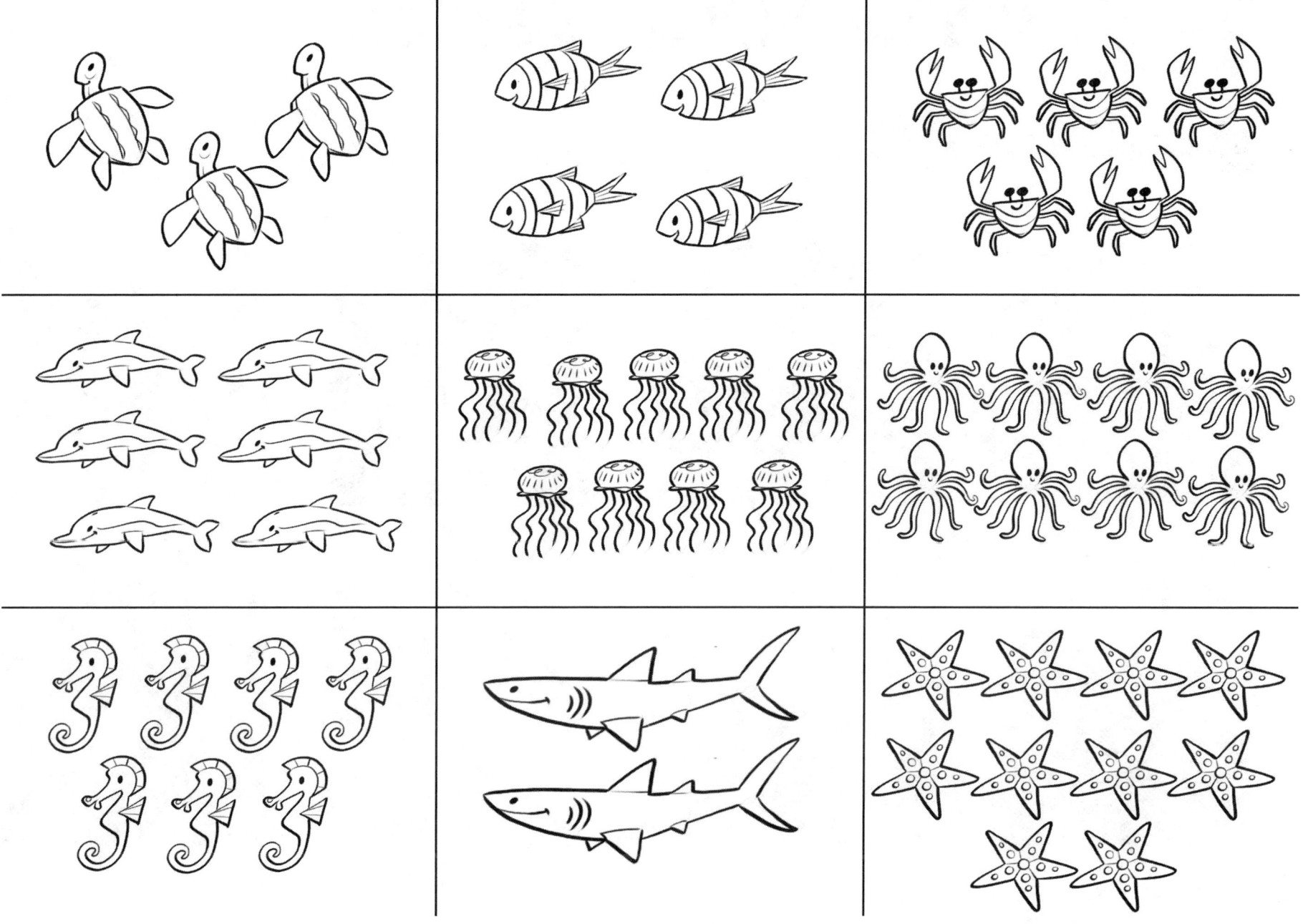

REVIEW: NEW WORDS: *crab, dolphin, jellyfish, octopus, seahorse, shark, starfish, turtle*
STRUCTURE: *How many crabs are there? There are fourteen crabs.*

57

UNIT 10 PICNIC TIME

1 TR: 10.1 Listen. Write ✔ or ✘.

1 ☐ 2 ☐ 3 ☐ 4 ☐

5 ☐ 6 ☐ 7 ☐ 8 ☐

2 Point and say.

NEW WORDS: *cheese, fruit, juice, lemonade, sandwich, picnic, vegetables, yogurt*

1

2

3

4

5

6

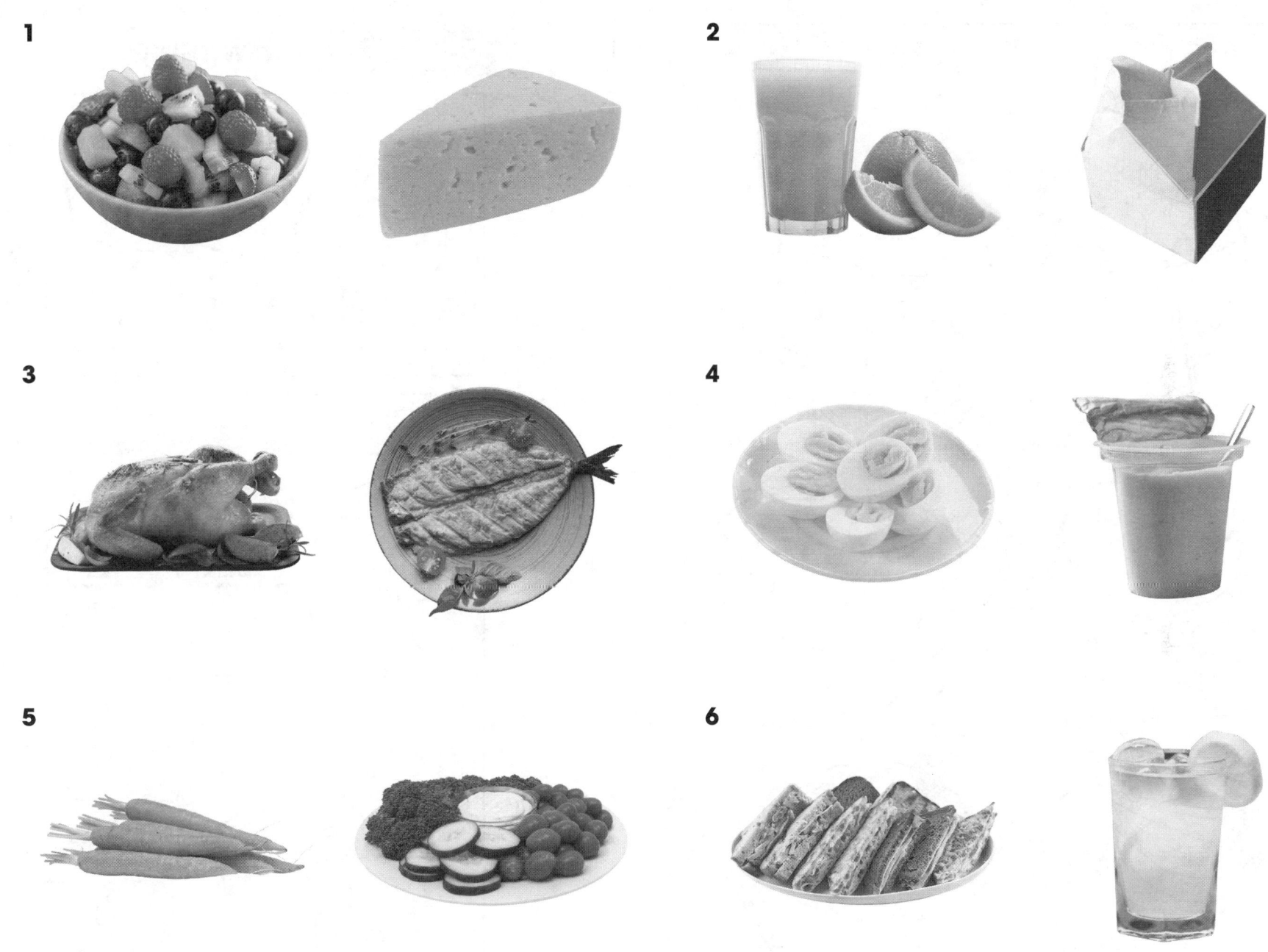

STRUCTURE: *Do you like fruit? Yes, I do./No, I don't.*

1 **TR: 10.3** Listen and color.

2 Write ✔ or ✗.

VALUE   TRY NEW THINGS.

1 ☐

2 ☐

3 ☐

1 TR: 10.4 Listen and trace. Say.

2 Trace.

1

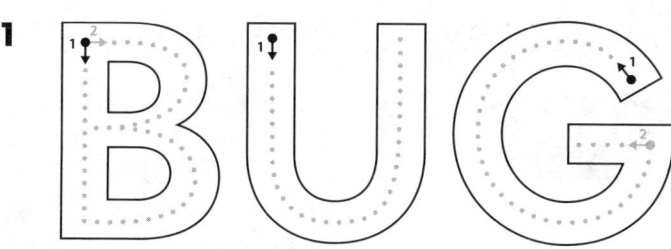

BUG

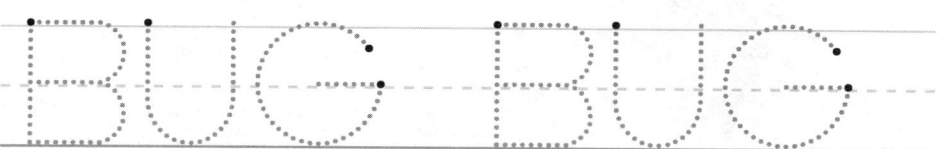

2

MUG

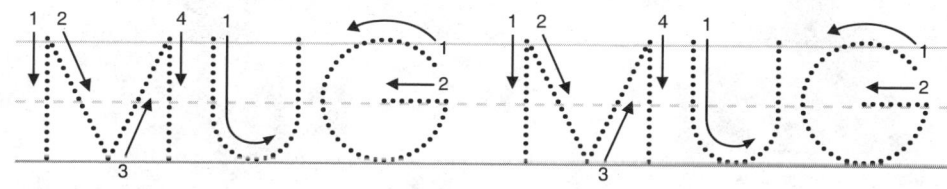

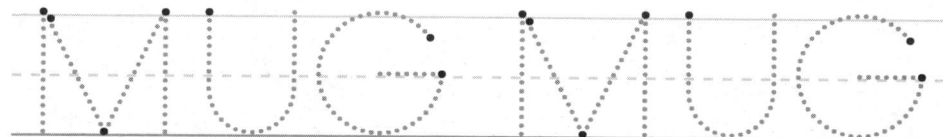

1 Color. Draw and say.

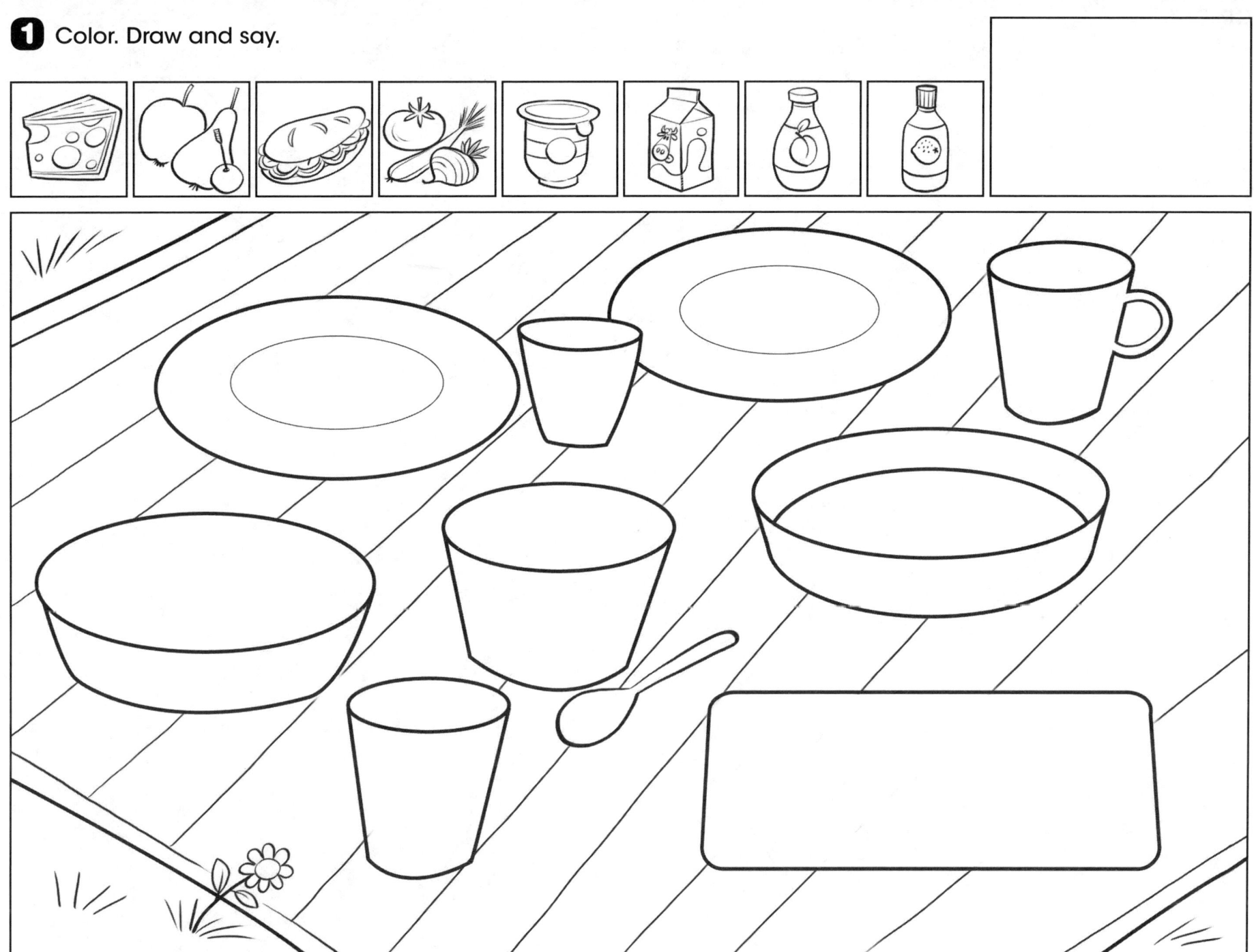

REVIEW: NEW WORDS: *cheese, fruit, juice, lemonade, picnic, sandwich, vegetables, yogurt*
STRUCTURE: *Do you like fruit? Yes, I do./No, I don't.*

63

CREDITS